THE MYSTERY OF THE HUMAN AURA

THE
MYSTERY
OF THE
HUMAN AURA

Ursula Roberts

Samuel Weiser, Inc.
York Beach, Maine

First published in England in 1950 by
The Spiritualist Association of Great Britain

First American Edition in 1977 by
Samuel Weiser, Inc.
Box 612
York Beach, ME, 03910

ISBN 0-87728-331-1

This revised edition, 1984

Printed in the United States by
Mitchell-Shear, Ann Arbor, MI

CONTENTS

THE MYSTERY OF THE HUMAN AURA

CHAPTER I

WHAT IS THE AURA?

THE AURA is defined as a magnetic field of vibration which surrounds every person, in the same way that light surrounds a lighted candle or perfume surrounds a flower. It is popularly described as an egg-shaped, vari-coloured field of vibration which radiates in all directions from the human form.

Symbolically, these radiations can be defined as the field of electricity which every individual manufactures from the materials at its disposal. As a dynamo utilizes the latent steam power, so the human machine can be said to utilize the electricity latent in other substances, converting them into the necessary energy needed for the exertions of daily life, hence the necessity for correct food, pure air and pure water. An insufficient supply of any one of these constituents will result in a measure of discomfort, and in course of time will bring about a state of illness. We may, therefore, conclude that the auric electricity is received by the human organism from natural sources and converted into the energy which drives the machine of the body.

The argument may be here advanced that the food used for human consumption differs in a vast degree from the mineral substances used in the production of electricty. Basically, the vegetable and the mineral kingdoms are identical. The analyst will prove that a given quantity of vegetable matter contains a percentage of mineral salts in varying quantities and of various kinds. In horticulture, it is customary to feed plants with inorganic chemical compounds, which, by a process of assimilation, change the basic colour of the flower, or produce variegation in the foliage. It is common knowledge that a hydrangea will produce richly coloured flowers if fed with a solution containing iron.

Spinach contains iron in such a form as to be easily assimilated by a body lacking in iron, and therefore lacking a substance needed for the manufacture of essential energy. A person lacking in the needful mineral matter becomes anæmic, easily tired and indulges in lengthy periods of sleep, during which time the minimum amount of electricity is needed for the functions of the human machine. An excess of organic substances will create what may be termed short-circuits, or explosive tendencies in the individual such as hysteria, apoplexy, and short temper.

We are accustomed to relegate periods of depression, headache and indigestion to digestive causes. We do not think sufficiently deeply to discover how and why certain foods affect the flow of our energy. It has been scientifically proved that the human machine can be maintained in a state of perfect health by a simple diet of uncooked vegetables, fruits, cereals, nuts and barks. All of these, upon analysis, reveal balanced quantities of easily digested mineral matter, whereas cooked and manufactured foods contain less quantities of these important substances. Dietetic research has proved that a low state of energy results from such diets.

We are, therefore, forced to the conclusion that it is not merely the amount of food which gives us energy, but the quality of the food and the time allowed for its assimilation, not merely into the blood-stream, but also into the electrical force from which our energy is derived. If it were food, air and water alone which maintained our life, we could safely consider that life could be prolonged indefinitely. When death occurs something in the human machine fails to assimilate the materials placed at its disposal, and therefore, the energy needed for normal functions becomes non-existent. A doctor can certify the cause of death as one of many diseases affecting given organs of the body, but he cannot certify with any degree of accuracy when and how the body first became prone to the disease, and why disease should appear in one person and not in another.

It has been proved, by observation, that disease shows itself in the aura *before* making itself felt in the organs of the physical body ; it can be seen as dark patches, or as a mottled condition in the vari-coloured radiation surrounding the individual, proving that some disorganization of the electrical field also takes place when disease is imminent.

Evidences that medical science is gradually coming to realize the electrical nature of man's constitution can be observed by the part that electrical therapy plays in the modern hospitals and specialists' consulting-rooms. As yet, the majority of doctors regard only the effects of electrical treament as shown by the response of the physical organs ; they work on the theory that certain electrical rays stimulate some bacteria and destroy others.

A few scientists have branched out into the theory that it is man's own electricity that reacts upon himself, and by the study of the aura are advancing slowly into a new theoretical idea of the cause of disease, an idea that has been aided by the invention of the Kilnascreen and the verification of clairvoyants that disease is shown in the aura before the onset of an illness, that the condition intensifies during illness and fades in convalescence, but leaves behind it a permanent imprint on the electrical field.

Dr. Alexander Cannon, who has investigated the unseen self of man through the medium of hypnotized clairvoyante subjects, states that the aura is composed of myriads of threadlike lines of force. It appears very probable that a condition of illness would deflect the flow of electricity along these lines, and after recovery some of them would remain permanently deflected, thus showing the imprint of past diseases and present weaknesses. It seems but a small step to the time when cures for all diseases will be discovered by the observation of the auric reactions to the various electrical rays.

In past ages we have evidence that men were dimly aware of the electrical force in vegetation and metals. Many of the amulets worn by superstitious people can be proved as possessing a high electrical potency. The idea that the amber necklace or ornament was the protector of good health can be seen as possessing a sound reason, since by friction amber will produce static electricity such as is sometimes used in electrical therapy. It is easy to see that the amber, in the process of wear would receive friction from the movements of the wearer, either against the skin or against the clothing, and would cast forth some of the electrical force so derived into the aura of the wearer, and, no doubt, make good some vibratory deficiency.

There is no doubt about the fact that mankind radiates this electricty, but no scientist up to the present time has been able to define electricity in exact terms, therefore nobody is able to state whether man's electricity is different from that which is harnessed for commercial and utilitarian purposes. The measure of electricity is in its reaction upon substances. It produces heat and light. When harnessed to the correct objects it can produce tremendous energy.

Man's electricity produces heat in his body, the capacity to register light waves in the eye, the necessary energy to breathe the essential ethers ; to keep the heart beating, and to produce thought and movement. It would appear that the electrical power is basically identical, but man varies in his use and assimilation of the power, as the Wimshurst machine differs from the enormous dynamos of the power stations which supply whole areas of the countryside with electricity.

Let us consider the terrific vital powers of natives living in their own environment ; of the hardy Scots and colonials.

All of these people, traditionally, eat sparsely of the natural products of the earth, unvitiated by commercial manufacturing processes. They work mainly out-of-doors, where the electrical power in the air is unconsciously utilized.

The fact that the force in the air *can* be utilized by the human machine is evidenced by the various phenomena of Yoga and its attendant sciences, all of which are based on the control of the breathing apparatus, through which alone the air force can be converted into human force. Here we stand on the verge of a vast, little-explored realm of science. We know that all the marvels of the East, such as levitations, fire-walking, stopping of the heart-beats and so forth, are prefaced by breath practice (*pranayama*) and selected practices for the strengthening of the will power. By these means the electrical force generated by the breathing exercises, concentrated in the aura, is directed to serve specific purposes, such as the production of seemingly abnormal phenomena.

Around the Yogis grow an ever-lengthening stream of stories. We hear about their endurance under conditions of privation ; their feats of energy, such as traversing tremendous distances on foot ; their ability to withstand the onslaught of diseases which would kill the man nourished upon the devitalized foods sold in our cities.

Many reasons may be advanced to confound these statements. They can be grouped under headings such as these : The difference in the diets is merely that of supplying different chemical constituents to the blood-stream ; the digestive powers vary according to the life of the individual ; or the out-of-door man absorbs an extra supply of ultra-violet through the pores of his skin, and of oxygen through his lungs, which enriches the blood-stream. These arguments do not destroy our electronic knowledge, for Professor Oscar Brunnler, among other eminent researchers into the world of radiations, states that a single drop of human blood has its own distinct field of radiation, as all other substances have, which he has investigated.

CHAPTER II

THE FORMATION OF THE AURA

THE NEWLY born infant may aptly be called an individualized fœtus, for with the first breath the infant draws it becomes something more than a collection of chemical accretions. It becomes an individualized personality, with all the potentialities of the man or woman it will later become.

As it holds in itself the potentialities of seeing, hearing, tasting, touching and smelling, so also does it hold in itself the potentialities of the electrical field called the aura, upon the development of which much of its growth and health will depend. It is significant that not until the first breath is drawn does the fœtus develop the first sign of auric radiation. Whether the actual soul is connected with the fœtus at the time of birth, or at the time of conception, is a detail which yet remains to be proved. We only know that with the first breath there appears round the infant the first hint of the aura, leading us to the conclusion that the aura is composed of matter, or radiation, drawn from the ethers in the atmosphere, which, when absorbed into the system, is again radiated forth in the form known as the aura.

This infantile aura has very much the same appearance as the infinity of atmosphere perceived by the human eye when looking into the immensity of the clear sky, and we believe that it is identically the same. As a magnet attracts corres- ponding substances within its field of vibration, so does the human spirit draw to itself some substance from the universal ether. This same substance increases in magnetic velocity and in course of time attracts other radiations which will form the adult aura. The atmosphere is in reality colourless, yet takes on a tinge of blue by reason of its immensity. The aura of an infant is colourless at the time of its birth, but gradually, through the months of its growth, it takes on a faint silvery- blue sheen which grows more marked towards the end of the first year, when intelligence begins to manifest in a definite form.

We call this aura the etheric sheath or the astral envelope, because it appears that all later developments take place within this subtle, indefinable area. This particular sheath is as in- definable as air and is rarely perceived by clairvoyants, though they may easily perceive other auric characteristics. It is the sheath known in mystical nomenclature as the garment of the soul, and such in truth it is, because it literally clothes the soul, which is expressing itself through the body of flesh in a sheath-like veil which, literally, is woven of the substance of space. Space itself may be but a garment of God, but to us it signifies the ineffable, glorious wonder of supernal Spirit, the medium by which we may most easily visualize That which cannot be visualized.

By some sects this auric garment is called the causal body, in that it appears to be the cause of all that follows in the life of the incarnate person, and, in the case of the person who develops a high degree of spirituality, this sheath glows with a supernal, unearthly radiance in which the ordinary auric vibrations glow with the sweet-pea delicacy of colourings. From clairvoyant observation, such an aura can be best des- cribed as a lucent bubble filled with coloured smokes, in the centre of which stands the physical body, from which these same colours stream in ever varying streams of light and shade.

It would appear that this causal sheath is built by the action of breathing, therefore it must be drawn from the sun-impregnated air, or the God-filled atmosphere we know as space. It is significant to note the improvement in the physique of children who, as babes, have spent long hours in the out-of-doors, in comparison with the practice, not many years ago, of confining infants to the house on all but the finest of days, with corresponding stunting of their growth. Who can say what race of super-men and women may not be produced in the future by our increased knowledge, not only of dietetics, but also of the needs of these other bodies, which, from a purely spiritual point of view, are even more important than the physical ones ? We can observe, also, the effects that correct breathing, as conducted in the physical culture classes, has had upon the physique of ordinary young men and women. It appears to the author that the results are out of all pro-portion to the simplicity of the practice, unless we take into consideration the fact that the air is charged with the divine life force of God.

To return to the causal body. This is the only aura to be perceived around the young infant. During the first months of life it appears to glow and palpitate with vibrations of extraordinary rapidity. From observation, one concludes that the whole purpose of the life of the infant is to attract all the available material for the building of a sound body. During the frequent periods of sleep a terrific work of construction appears to go forward in this aura. It is a truism to say that the first months of life can make or mar the well-being of a person for ever, and we may well conclude that in the case of an infant whose digestive processes are marred by improper food or care, resulting in interruptions of the sleep periods, this building of the causal body will be interrupted. The other processes which are dependent upon it will, in course of time, be less perfect.

From the ninth to the eighteenth month a gradual change can be noticed in the aura. The bubble-like sheath becomes gradually filled with a beautiful blue vibration which seems to emanate from the pores of the skin of the young child and surround him in a moving cloud of cloudy matter. This blue radiation is entirely an individual creation, and varies according to the temperament of the child. In the case of a weakly child the blue is of a fainter colour than that of a child whose intense activity and intelligence result in a deep shade of glorious colour.

The ailments and constitutional weaknesses of the young children can be discovered in this blue field as patches of greyish colouring, imposed upon the blue in the area of the ailment. Thus, a cold or cough would betray a grey patch in the area of the lungs, and in the region of the head if the sinus, ears or eyes were affected. In the region of the stomach the aura discloses digestive disorders and so forth.

This blue aura we have come to call the health aura, though sometimes it is called the etheric sheath. It remains with the individual from the time of childhood to the time of death, and upon it are imposed the health and disease reactions of the whole lifetime. Upon its blueness or greyness depend the general well-being of the grown individual. It is a certain indication of the general health, and its symptoms should never be ignored. A disability may well show itself in this aura before manifesting in the physical body as actual disease.

It is obviously an emanation manufactured by the blood-stream, since it is radiated from every part of the body. The medical profession leads us to believe that good health depends largely upon the supply of iron in the blood-stream. We might conclude from this that possibly it is the iron content of the blood which emits the blue vibration. It remains but for science to verify or nullify the theory. Be that as it may, an anæmic, iron-deficient person radiates a poor health aura ; the improvement can be observed when such iron deficiency is made good.

The aura of the infant gradually takes on this blue tinge as the food becomes assimilated into the system, but at birth it is of so faint a nature that it scarcely colours the globe of the causal body. When the weaning period begins and the babe starts to take foods other than milk, the deepening in colour can be marked as a rapid, fluctuating process ; the blue intensifies during the period following a meal and decreases as hunger approaches. We do not, at present, know why this should be so, but we know the rapidity with which children lose weight and energy ; perhaps it is that the vibrations of the blood-stream and the aura become dissipated with a corresponding rapidity.

After the first year another change begins to be seen in the aura. A faint, rosy tinge is perceived in the midst of the blue vibration ; a tinge which appears to emanate from the region of the solar plexus. This vibration very slowly spreads and intensifies in colour until about the age of five, when another change can also be observed. The writer believes this to be the colour of the natural instincts and appetites, since it can be seen to intensify to a deep red when the child is provoked to anger, and dying to the original pink when the interest is diverted. Possibly it is created by the different substances extracted from the food on which the child is fed. We all know that certain foods, by creating digestive difficulties, can also upset the nervous system. We may conclude that the introduction of high protein-valued foods create a different nervous radiation which is shown aurically in this manner.

One must conclude that the red radiation is of nervous and emotional origin since it is situated in the region of the solar plexus. It is well known that all emotions affect the nervous system which radiates from the plexus centre in the same way that railway lines may radiate across the country from a certain terminus. It is also known that people who live upon a diet composed largely of animal food have proverbially unstable nervous systems in which animal passions such as lust, greed, anger, etc., are apt to overpower the reasoning faculties. We must conclude that the constituents in animal foods supply to the human organism a high rate of nervous energy which is thrown off in this manner. It has been ob-served in the case of vegetarians that the plexus radiation is of a soft pink shade, in contrast to that of the flesh eater, who betrays a red which differs in the degree of murkiness accor-ding to the amount of the food consumed. The radiation also differs in its colouring according to the temperament of the individual. Thus a calm, self-controlled person radiates a soft and gentle red, while the hasty tempered and lustful tempera-ment betrays shades of crimson or scarlet.

Again we must return to the topic of food. It has been frequently proved that a change in diet results in a change of temper ; much ill temper is known to be seated in digestive disturbances, through diets which supply too much protein to the system, causing blood-pressure and choleric outbursts. In the case of children, this radiation appears as a normal stage in their development ; it is undoubtedly rooted in some dietary change, but it is indicative of natural instincts such as hunger, adventure, anger, curiosity, affection, etc., without the experience of which it would not, as it does, evolve the in-tellectual, thinking self.

The sensitive child is invariably the child who is not very strong physically and in the sensitive, nervous child both the blue and the pink radiations are far more subtle than in the case of the robust child, whose explosive interest in all things, and whose practically inexhaustible energy, betrays the depth of the blue and red colourings. Again I return to the food question and point out that the delicate child is naturally fed with finer, milkier and more easily digested food that the child who can digest anything suitable to its years, in consequence of which the nervous radiations would differ in the materials from which they originated.

In later years, when the adult begins the spiritual quest, it is the sensitive individual who easily subdues the animal nature and cleanses the consciousness of earthly desires pre-paratory to Illumination, while the passionate man or woman struggles long and hard to control the elements which have been built into their make-up during childhood.

We believe that the world of the future will be peopled by men and women with giant intellects, illumined by spiritual understanding. We can see the trend of this development in the modern interest in metaphysical ideals, and in the wide-spread food reform movement.

CHAPTER III

THE DAWN OF INTELLECT

THE DAWN of the intellect can be seen in the aura of the child by the appearance of a faint yellow glow in the region of the head. At first it is no more than an ethereal cloud of palest lemon, into which rays of deeper yellow occasionally shoot as an effort at reasoning is made by the child. This radiation usually makes its appearance about the age of seven years, but in the case of a precocious child it might appear earlier. It is entirely associated with the thinking capacity.

Those persons who have studied children and who understand them, will agree that very few children actually reason, to any extent, before the age of five to seven years. Up to that age the child acts by instinct and by imitation ; later it learns by experience to weigh the results of its actions, desisting from some things because it can see a reason why those things should be avoided, whereas before it desisted because it was ordered to do so. The process of life up to the time of this change is entirely one of absorption. The child absorbs impressions, knowledge, likes and dislikes, food and air, in the same way as a sponge absorbs water. Once the process of absorption is complete, however, a new process takes place. Some of the food elements become active in the brain, and the child begins to think. The more he thinks, the more elements are used by the brain and the brighter becomes the radiation.

We know that the child who is forced to study for too long a time rapidly becomes thin and anæmic. The reason is simple, in that the elements of air, food and sunlight cannot be utilized for all purposes at once. If the child is using the brain and transmuting life force into intellect, it cannot at the same time use it for other necessary purposes, hence the necessity for a balanced curriculum in the life of every child. The development should be balanced between brain, instinct and emotion. It should be considered more necessary to produce an adult who is fully developed in every way, than to produce an adult who is the perfect product of a particular system and who conforms to a certain preconceived pattern ; who possesses a certain knowledge of all the things which his forbears have decided necessary and which probably will never be useful to him in his ordinary life.

Identical with the appearance of this thinking radiation is the tendency of the child to develop egoity. There comes also a marked change in the manner of speech, which alters from the reflective to the personal. Thus the reflective personality, reflecting those around him, will say : " Johnny wants an apple," but will now change to the personal, " I want an apple." The process of the development of intellect brings to the child a sense of its own individuality and separateness from the world around ; the process is so gradual that for long periods the reflective personality will be uppermost and parents are startled when the personal aspect suddenly shows itself by very definite demands.

Some children have this intellectual radiation more clearly marked than others. It is this type of child who becomes a " Book-worm " ; who avidly devours knowledge and becomes the man or woman of intellect. In the normal child, living in an ordinary environment, this yellow does not become so intense in colour as the red of the passional body or the blue of the health body. In the case of the mentally deficient child this radiation is practically non-existent, though it may be developed by careful training. The mentally deficient child, or adult, alternates between moods of rage and excessive affec-tion, both of which belong to the passional nature. The reflective nature is still largely in operation in cases of this kind and can be observed from the imitative tendencies of the imbecile.

This intellectual radiation is also produced from the chemical matter circulated by the blood-stream. We know that eggs, fish and milk are the best forms of food for the people who work with their brain ; the general idea is that they are more easily digested, but they are also rich in phos-phorus, proteins and iron, which, when conveyed to the brain canals, obviously produce the correct reactions.

We all know the difficulty experienced after a heavy meal, when an air of heaviness weighs upon the mind and creative work becomes difficult, if not impossible. It is interesting, from the view-point of a clairvoyant, that after a heavy meal the radiation around the head is apt to grow a little dim, while the solar plexus activity increases as the food is digested and the voluntary nervous system does its work. This may explain why the best creative work is invariably produced at night or very early in the morning. Authors and musicians are noted for their burning of the midnight oil. It may be partially due to the quietness of the world at that time, but is more likely to be due to the fact that the meals have been digested and the whole energy of the body can be utilized by the brain.

In the case of the creative worker the radiation around the head sometimes assumes a most wonderful luminosity, which extends its field of light around the head and shoulders, com-pletely blotting out all other radiations in the area. In this field of light will flash other colours according to the type of thought the work produces in the mind of the artist. Thus, work of an uplifting nature, such as the writing of a poem or the painting of a religious picture, will produce waves of beautiful purples and blues. Work of an intellectual nature, associated merely with mundane affairs, such as the writing of letters, totalling of ledgers, etc., will produce an intense but rather hard shade of orange or yellow. The musician, playing a work with genuine feeling and entering into the spirit of the composition, will show corresponding colours in the aura, thus a pink or blue for emotional music, green for soothing, pastoral bars, and deep purples, blues and golds for the grand music of a Beethoven, Bach or Brahms.

It is this mental aura which betrays the true personality of a man or woman, for here is imprinted a record of the type of thought most frequently held in the mind. An intelligent observer can watch the red of lustful thoughts, the scarlet flash of anger, the yellow-green of jealousy flashing across the yellow field of the aura and betraying the ideas that lie behind the pleasant talk and polished manner of an acquaintance. Another time one might sit in a church and watch the wonderful shades of mauve sweeping over the aura as a person is uplifted by something in the service which touches the heart; or one may see the blue of love as some damsel sees the man of her hopes, or watch the irritable flashes of harsh yellow and red as another person criticizes the sermon, the choir or the neighbours.

It is interesting to note that types of thought which are held for any length of time tend to set up a permanent hint of colour in the aura, so that the pure yellow of intellect becomes dyed with the reds, blues, greens and mauves of the predominating thoughts, and we can tell, by this same vibration, that one person is of a generous disposition, another of an avaricious nature; one is spiritually inclined and another thinks of nothing but worldly success in connection with business.

The changes wrought by the psychologists, who work under the assumption that the thought deliberately held for any length of time in the mind will eventually affect the general character of an individual, is here again proved correct, for clairvoyant observation proves the power of a thought to colour the auric field so thoroughly that it ceases to be yellow and will become bluish, if the thinker is of a devotional nature. Reddish-brown predominates in a sensual thinker, and slate-grey in a person continually in the habit of thinking in a depressed and hopeless manner.

If we possess a will of sufficient strength, there is nothing we cannot do with this mental aura. We can transmute it to any shade of colour we wish. The majority of people allow themselves to be possessed by their moods and thoughts, instead of thinking what *they* will and radiating the kind of vibration *they* choose. Many of us have a desire to create beauty. Most people think that they could paint wonderful pictures or create marvellous images. They do not realise that the people who create these things first of all create beauty, law and order in their own minds, resulting in the ability to create external beauty.

To all who feel that they could create, had they but the opportunity, I say : First create beauty in yourself by the thinking of beautiful thoughts. Paint on the screen of your own aura with the brush of your own mind and you will be surprised at the opportunities which life will bring to you. You will be amazed at the latent gifts in your character which will spring to new life and blossom into external beauty. Everyone has a mental aura and they can make of it what they will. It begins with the clear yellow of childhood and it may end with the glorious, glowing colour of a saint, or the lowering colours of resentment, hatred and depression. In this field, more than any other in the aura, a man or woman has a free choice as to whatever he or she chooses to create. It is never too late to begin the changing process and to transmute the base colour into the gold of spirituality.

CHAPTER IV

TYPES OF AURA

TO CLAIRVOYANT vision the aura appears as a mass of palpitant colour which differs in colouring and size with each individual. It betrays with unerring accuracy the habits, thoughts and diseases of each person. The generous person has an expansive, softly coloured aura. The miser has a murky, contracted aura. The sensualist has a scarlet and crimson field of radiation ; the business man, with no thought above worldly success, has an aura of orange tint. The devotee has one of mauve or blue and the saint a dazzling mother-of-pearl light which radiates to a distance of several feet around him. The ordinary person, who is neither very good nor very bad, has an aura of medium size, radiating to a distance of about two feet and showing colouring that is sometimes radiant, sometimes murky, according to their mood.

How do the colours change from the triple foundation of childhood to the multiplicity of adulthood ? In childhood the whole aura is volatile ; one moment the head colour will be predominant and another the red of the passional nature. The whole nature of childhood is that of flux and change.

The adult must of necessity become set in his habit and steady in his thought. He must control the changing moods and learn the art of concentration, by means of which the changing vibrations will become concentrated into certain areas and a bias be made in favour of a certain colour expressive of the predominating traits.

In the case of the business man, whose sole ambition is connected with the promotion of worldly interests, much of his vital power must of necessity become concentrated into the area of the intellect. He is forced to use his mind to think, to plan, to weigh the consequences of every action, with the result that he will develop the head aura to such an extent that it will dominate the emotional aura, and the mixture of yellow and red will result in a bright shade of orange. The man or woman who will give their friendship or affection only if it appeals to their business instincts, will show a vibration similar to this. The saying : " He loves with his head," develops a very literal meaning, since part of the emotional colouring becomes drawn into the head colouring.

The aura of the miser is typical of his nature, in which all the natural instincts are concentrated into the one channel of greed, which is associated with the passional nature. Consequently the aura becomes very small, hard in outline and harsh in colouring. Instead of the vibrations radiating freely around him, they are drawn into one focal centre. All the faculties of the intellect are bent upon the passion of acquisition and in course of time the yellow of the intellect becomes drawn into the red of the passional nature. All the colours are harsh and murky ; they combine to form a dirty shade of brownish-orange, while the outer edge of the aura, through being constantly drawn inwards to its centre, ceases to cast off surplus matter and develops what appears as a hard crust, which completely encloses the person. Through this crust it is almost impossible to penetrate, hence the difficulty of reasoning with such a person or of attempting to arouse in them some higher feeling.

The state of such a person is most pitiable, for when we lay down the physical body, consciousness continues within the auric body. If the auric body is encased in a hard shell nobody can break through it to approach him, with the result that the person will suffer intense feelings both of loneliness and helplessness. Nobody can free a person so encased except the person who has created the casing. It behooves us, there- fore, for our comfort, not only in this world, but also in the next, to cultivate habits of cheerfulness and of generosity. Let us give freely of our love ; our slight knowledge ; our personal possessions, if we have any, so that we may develop an aura expanded by love and radiating around us in soft shades of rose-pink, pale blue, lemon or *eau-de-nil*. When we develop broad-mindedness and generosity, the red element in our aura becomes changed to rose-pink. If the person is of a religious nature it changes to blue. The mind aura becomes expanded when we use it to think of other people's needs, and coloured with blue in the amount of love with which we so concern ourselves.

The colour of earthly love is red, being rooted in the sex nature, and the aura of a sensual man or woman is flooded by warm tones of crimson, scarlet and blue. The blue is of a deep rather dirty shade, which at times appears almost purple when mixed with the red. Such a person shows very little intellectual light, because all the powers are focussed in the centre of emotion. They feel, rather than think, and their life is ruled not by reason, but by desire. Sometimes, however, such people conceive strong attachments for their children, or some cir- cumstance arises in which they are forced to curb the desire- nature and love more unselfishly. It is then interesting to notice the gradual shifting of the focus of vibration from the region of the sex organs to the centre of the heart, with a corresponding refinement in colouring. Intense shades of harsh reds change to soft rose and finally to glorious blue.

The intensity with which such people can love when the emotions are transmuted to a higher centre, such as the heart, may in time transform them from sinners into saints ; for upon our capacity to love depends our own spiritual advance ment. We might say, too, that upon our capacity to love depends the salvation of all humankind, for it is the law that real love must of necessity draw a response from the persons loved, and they in turn will love, becoming also miniature saviours of humankind.

The saints of this world, what of them ? The saints who dwell in little slum apartments ; the saints of cottages with small backyards and enormous families of children, some of which have been adopted from even less fortunate circum stances ? The saints who spend their lives scrubbing, cooking, praying, nursing the infant and the aged ; loving everybody indiscriminately, what of them ?

I wish you could catch just one glimpse of such an aura, in which all the colours seem to vibrate from the centre of the heart. The red of the passions has been lifted up and changed to flashing shades of azure and sapphire, which inter penetrate what is left of the passional nature, so that it appears mauve, and the colour of the intellect, which plans and thinks for others, is charged with these same shades of blue, so that it appears sometimes as blue, sometimes eau-de-nil, sometimes lemon. The glory of such colourings, when perceived in surroundings bereft of beauty and surrounding a person who may be utterly illiterate, makes one feel very humble, for here is a literal example of how the glory of God is attained by merit only and not by wealth, position or knowledge.

Then there are the saints of another world. The saints who give their lives to teach the ignorant ; to heal the sick ; who grow weary in the service of humanity and who ask no reward except that the mystical grace of God illumine their lives. These people develop an aura wherein the heart and the head centres become equally active. Such persons have studied and attained knowledge to fit them for their tasks, therefore the intellect radiates a glorious glow of yellow which changes to white during moments of extreme exaltation, and lemon or blue in moments of love. Most of the passional nature becomes concentrated into the region of the heart, which vibrates beautiful tones of mauve, purple or blue according to the mood. Auras such as this can only belong to the lovers of humanity, not merely those who serve because they have been trained for a vocation.

Needless to say, every aura differs from another, for one man will love more than another who thinks, and he who thinks may at times love very greatly. It is auras such as these that may eventually expand into the glorious mother-of-pearl of the illumined mahatma, saint or teacher, who will leave such a mark on the history of the world that even the sands of time will have difficulty in effacing it.

With such souls a mysterious moment is attained in which another centre, situated in the top of the head, becomes active and its radiation touches the faint, silvery shell of the casual body, which immediately penetrates the ordinary aura, flooding it with silvery radiance, so that the colours there become luminous with new light and new beauty. The saint becomes not a saint of this world, but a saint of the heavenly world and his or her work, thenceforth, is a work supernal. His or her sojourn in this world is a sojourn of outstanding beauty. It is the attainment not only of a purified consciousness, but of a super-consciousness, and such a person remains for ever a super-man or a super-woman.

CHAPTER V

DISEASE AND THE AURA

THE HEALERS, who have been able to cure diseases of the physical body by working through the aura, are apt to regard the disease as caused by the auric vibration, instead of the auric field registering disease, as the outcome of some-thing in the physical make-up. By healers, I mean all those people who have come to admit the reality of the aura, both by observation and experimentation.

It would appear that the aura gives a true picture of every element which is in the human organism. If the food, as it is assimilated into the various centres, radiates its particular magnetic power into the aura, correspondingly a lack of certain substances will betray a weakening of this same aura, so that a person suffering from nervous debility will show an aura pale in colouring and tinged with grey. A cancerous person betrays an excess of vibration in the region of the cancer, since the growth itself is composed of organic matter which has its own individual field of vibration. The ills of man are too numerous to mention and the cures for the ills of man are almost as numerous. Which of the cures are the best ? We can only think that the cure which gives the best and the most lasting result is the best cure. We should become like the Chinese, and keep our healers for the prevention of our ailments, not for the cure of them.

In the future, I do not doubt but that there will be clinics in every town where the aura can be periodically examined for traces of disease, and instead of diagnosing by following the dim pathways of half-remembered pains, which may indicate a twinge of rheumatism, a cancer, or a muscle over-exerted, the healers will definitely be able to read the history of each person, as a doctor reads a hospital chart, and act accordingly. In such clinics, disease will be treated before it has time to become a chronic condition. Thousands of pounds will then be available for the education, housing and uplifting of people's minds instead of being used to maintain homes for the incurable, clinics for half-incurables, and hospitals for the sick and neglected bodies of ignorant humanity.

In these present years the surgeon's knife is a necessity, because disease has invariably been allowed to progress to a pitch when no other means can adequately deal with it, but we cannot believe that the Maker endowed us with organs so securely protected by layers of skin, muscle and bone if it was also intended that the same flesh should be opened for the treatment of disease.

At present, the herbalist appears to be the person who most satisfactorily approaches the ideal of the perfect healer, since his herbs, each with their own individual magnetic vibration, become assimilated into the human body and supply to it certain substances which may be lacking. The whole art of healing consists merely in re-establishing balance and harmony. Any method, therefore, whether it is of diet or of medicine, which tends to alter the vibratory rate of the body, must be in accordance with the laws of healing. Methods which necessitate violent shocks to the system, as in the case of even the simplest operation, cannot be good, since, though they remove the main seat of the disease, they upset the whole harmony and balance of the physical and auric bodies. The time taken for recovery after a severe operation ; the broken effect which the aura betrays ; the weakness and anæmia, all prove that this is man's own method and not a method decreed by divine law.

It is interesting to notice the growth of unorthodox healing together with the growth of unorthodox thinking. Never have so many cults flourished as they flourish now. Spiritualism and Theosophy have prepared the way for cults which foster every metaphysical attribute possessed by man-kind.

Spiritual healing and nature cure lead the way for the cure of physical disease, but after them follow cults for the drinking of water ; for fasting ; for eating this, and not eating that ; for sitting in the rays of the sun, and for sitting in the rays of the moon ; for breathing, and for not breathing, until deluded humanity wonders whether it is not at the mercy of all the elements of nature, and I wonder that they do not revert to the simple heathen method of making propitiatory offerings to the primal powers in the forces of nature. All these cults have a dim remnant of truth in them, since each one aims at altering the vibratory effect of the human body. By fasting, certain elements become less active in the system. By drinking water, other elements are cleansed ; by exercise, the breathing is increased and impurities are cast forth in the form of perspiration and carbon dioxide.

Of late years a new technique of healing has made its appearance. Spiritualists and Christian Scientists have dis-covered a way to metaphysical healing which has yielded amazing results. Without the use of either drug, knife or herb, cripples have been cured and dying people brought to the ful-ness of health. Certain persons have been found whose radiations are of a slightly different nature to that of the ordinary person, and disease, on coming into the area of their magnetism, becomes transmuted into health. The Spiritualist healers have performed, and still are performing, amazing cures, merely by holding their hands in the area of the aura and transmitting this curative power. By touch and by prayer this great work goes forward.

It is interesting to watch such a healer at work on a tumour or a cancer, when, by certain movements of the hands in the area of the disease, the fungi-like mass of vibration becomes temporarily broken-up and dispersed into the main area of the aura, or in some cases is drawn out, by magnetic attraction, to the hands of the healer. This has a weakening effect upon the growth, and no doubt, in course of time, deprives it of life. There are countless authentic instances of cancer cures in the annals of the Spiritualist movement.

In diseases of exhaustion, such as nervous prostration, tuberculosis, etc., the aura of the patient appears to sop up the healing vibrations, as a damp sponge may absorb water, and a corresponding brightening of the electrical field can be observed. It appears that even as the physical body radiates electricity, so also can it absorb it, either from another person, from such natural sources as sun, air or water, or from machines manufactured for its transmission.

From various data the fact emerges that the human healer appears to radiate a power which is different from any other power, since cures by such means are recorded in which ordinary electrical treatment had failed to secure satisfactory results. We must, therefore, conclude that human electricity is a thing entirely individual to each man and woman, and in such healers as Mr. W. T. Parrish, Mr. Edwards, Mr. Steabben, to name but a few, we see it developed and utilized to the fulness of its extent. Jesus the Christ was the greatest exponent in history of the power by which human electricity, reacting upon the aura, can produce results in the physical body.

There is another aspect of Spiritualistic healing which must receive our consideration. In many cases the cures are attributed to the power brought by discarnate personalities known as guides, who transmit their own electrical radiations through the aura and the hands of the medium. It is interesting to watch the aura of a healer who works in this manner. In many cases the guide (the name for a discarnate personality) stands at a distance from the medium and projects what appears as rays from his own person. These rays strike the aura of the medium, causing it to acquire a new brilliancy of colouring and to increase in size. When the healer places his hands in the aura of the patient, these same rays become focussed into his hands and for a few minutes the patient, the healer, and the guide are linked into a unity by the waves of dazzling light which pass from one to another with incredible rapidity.

In absent healing, or healing by prayer, a similar process comes into operation. The healer concentrates his thought upon the patient, which creates a wave of electrical vibration between them both, and along this vibration healing power may be transmitted in a similar manner to that accomplished by touch, or the laying on of hands.

The interesting point about this type of healing lies in the fact that these discarnate souls, in spite of their tremendous compassion for suffering humanity, appear unable to transmit their healing without the aid of a medium. It seems that there must be an electrical affinity between the aura of the medium and the aura of the guide, and these, when combined, produce a vibration which is different from the ordinary vibrations associated with this world. We are only just beginning to understand the potency of these vibrations, by observing the results of such healing.

In considering this matter, the writer confesses to a feeling of intense humility. As a traveller must feel humble when he views from a mountain peak a vast, uncharted realm of wonderful beauty and amazing possibilities, so do I feel that we stand on the verge of a realm of blessedness which may produce a cure for all the ills of humankind ; a realm into which we have not as yet ventured. Only a few people have dared to stand on the verge and make slight sallies of exploration.

CHAPTER VI

PSYCHIC PHENOMENA

HOW DOES psychic phenomena affect the aura ? How does the aura affect psychic phenomena ? If these questions could be finally and scientifically answered, psychic phenomena could be produced almost at will. Unfortunately the exact answer still remains unknown, although the years of patient investigation by many people, both known and unknown, have produced a few basic facts and a few broad outlines along which other people are enabled to step forward a little more confidently. We know, for instance, that darkness is essential to the production of a good materialization ; that light waves have a destructive effect upon the substance known as ecto-plasm ; that a state of harmony between the medium and the sitters is essential to the production of all good phenomena ; we know that a medium is essential, and that really good mediums are very rare. We do not know in what degree the aura contributes to the power which is felt in good seances, and, for some unknown reasons, is entirely lacking in others.

The writer does not claim to express an opinion on this matter, nor in any way to lay claim to being an authority upon it. There are, however, one or two things which she has been able to gather from careful observation, and which are now presented in the hope that they may be of value to other people who have not had the same opportunities.

It would appear that all psychic phenomena depend to a great degree upon the sensitivity of the aura, or upon the power of the individual person to respond to the intangible world of vibratory forces such as thought, music, natural beauty, and the supernatural worlds which interpenetrate this world. People who are sensitive, people of artistic temperament ; the generous-hearted, loving type of person, all are open to the super-sensual world, but the person whose whole interest is turned inward to himself, the miser, the man or woman who imagines an insult in every word uttered by other people, such people are unlikely to receive outstanding personal psychical manifestations, for the simple reason that the aura is too insensitive to convey the vibrations to the physical brain.

When a discarnate soul—a mother, for instance, drawn by her intense love to a son or daughter—desires to make herself known, she has either to impinge her influence on to the aura or she has to pass through it in order to touch or otherwise make her presence known to her child. This passing through the aura is no easy matter. We must remember that she is functioning in a body composed mainly of matter similar to that of the aura, and therefore for her to pass through it would be analogous to any one of us trying to pass through the physical body of another. It just cannot be done. In an instance such as that of the mother and the child, the love link would enable the mother to overcome the difficulty and she would be able to impress an image of herself so strongly on the aura that her child would become aware of her presence.

A medium who develops a fine state of sensitivity to etheric vibrations, and who places his or her gifts at the service of humanity, works to a very definite plan. A guardian is placed in charge of his, or her, psychic development, and this guardian (or guide) interpenetrates the aura of the medium with his own vibratory force until the aura becomes doubly sensitive and quickly responsive to all super-sensual vibrations. He then transmits through the aura information concerning the discarnate souls who desire to contact their friends and relatives who are still tied to a physical body.

In the head of every person are two glands, known as the pituitary gland and the pineal gland. In some people these glands are active and in some they are dormant ; in some people they are fitfully active, but upon them depend the faculties of clear-seeing and clear-hearing. The pineal gland gives the power of registering the vibrations of the supernal world in the form of vision and the pituitary gland of registering the vibrations in the form of sound, and thus when the discarnate guardian projects his information into the aura of the medium, one of these two centres will respond and the medium will either see a vision or hear a voice.

Psychic communion is not the easy matter many people imagine it to be ; the slightest impression registered by the human brain has possibly been conveyed by an intricate process from the supernatural world, but many and marvellous things have been brought about by it. The hopeless have been given encouragement ; the would-be suicide has retained his life ; the sorrowful have been made glad, and in the future, I think man's salvation from his own greedy madness will be by the conscious use of this same power, through which he will be guided wisely to wield the affairs of nations with the help of great discarnate statesmen. He will be led to guard against war, epidemic and calamity, for the ramifications of mediumship extend from mere fortune-telling to the powers of prophecy ; from curing a cut finger to reading in the book of nature the cure and prevention of diseases such as cancer, bubonic plague, tuberculosis and sleeping-sickness.

At this time there are hundred of groups and organisations scattered over the world, most of which will aid anyone who so desires, to develop the psychic powers lying latent in their personality. There is nothing very mysterious about this process. The would-be medium is expected to sit with a group of people among whom there will be one, at least, who is a developed medium. They sit in chairs placed in a circular fashion round the room, so that if their hands are joined each person is in contact with the other and their auras will correspondingly interpenetrate.

The medium in charge, as we know, has an aura already sensitized by the guardian, and this same guide now transmits his power into the aura of the medium and it is then transmitted through the contact of his hands to the sitters on either side, whose auras become charged with as much of this power as they are able to receive ; they are also in contact with the other sitters and some of the power is transmitted through their hands until it has penetrated the whole of the circle, and for the time being should have the effect of sensitizing, in a greater or lesser degree, the auras of the sitters concerned. If any of these sitters have glands which are at all active, they should be able to register some of the sights or sounds of the supernatural world.

There are people who develop a degree of mediumship after an operation, illness or accident which affects the glands of the body. Natural psychics are those men and women who develop their powers as the natural outcome of the glandular changes at the age of puberty and middle-age, but it is invariably noticeable that they each have a guardian who is responsible for the further unfolding and steadying of their powers of registration. In the case of the medium who is fully awake to the supernal vibrations the aura betrays an extra vortex of activity in the region of the forehead, almost as if an extra auxiliary aura is active in the region of the pituitary and pineal glands.

There are many misconceptions concerning the power of the supernatural world over the mediums of this world, but in each and every case psychic phenomena are either projected

through the aura or produced in conjunction with the emana-
tions of the aura. Thus in trance mediumship, as it is invariably
called, the spirit entities are able to paralyse the functions of
the worldly intellect and superimpose over it their own ideas,
mannerisms and personalities in such a way that we see : not
the medium, but another personality speaking with the
medium's voice and moving the medium's limbs. A medium
can be used in this way for the transmission either of teaching,
writing, painting, inspiration or proof of continued identity
after death.

Many and wonderful are the manifestations that can be
produced, but we must not expect impossibilities. We have to
realize that the supernal world is different, in a vibratory
sense to this world, and if we want signs of the presence of
discarnate beings we must be willing to co-operate by developing the better side of our nature, from which will spring a
sensitive aura that will encourage, not repel, the loved ones
who wait to guide and guard us. Similarly we must not expect
impossibilities of our mediums when we go to them for help,
for our aura will aid the manifestations, or mar them. The aura
of the medium is super-sensitive, not only to the vibrations of
the supernatural world, but also to those of this world. If we
go to a medium who is known to be in touch with the " other
side " and we come away disappointed, we should invariably
blame ourselves for the disappointment. It is we who have
failed, and not the medium, nor the spirit world.

Another type of wonderful phenomena is classified under
the broad heading of physical phenomena. This includes
materialization, independent voice and levitation, phenomenon
through which the spirit world attunes itself to this world
and makes itself known in language which we cannot fail to
understand. By means of the substance known as ectoplasm,
the discarnate friend, relative or guide can clothe himself or
herself in a temporary garment out of which he can build a
body which appears as warm, as solid, as individualistic as the
one he possessed upon earth. Any person who has met a loved

one at a materialization seance, who has touched that same one, spoken to and heard the reply of that same one, can never again doubt that human personality survives the change called death ; the change that, in reality, leads to Life abundant, progressive and supernal.

This same ectoplasm can be built into an artificial larynx, by means of which the spirit entities can speak in voices audible to all. It can be formed into hands that may caress us, or levitate articles in the room about us, or transport objects from one place to another, with a view to proving that they are intelligent beings, and not mere blind forces acting in a manner contrary to the known laws of nature.

One of our best materializing mediums, Mrs. Helen Duncan, has suffered from many illnesses. She also enjoys a hearty meal before every seance takes place, and the writer holds the theory that the food, in view of the abnormal health condition, creates certain chemical substances which the spirit guides are able to withdraw by action through the aura, trans-muting them into ectoplasm.

The following analysis of ectoplasm was made by Baron Schrenck Notzing. His book, *Phenomena of Materialization*, is one of the most informative on this subject of ectoplasmic substances. Under the heading of Microscopic examination, he gave this description : " Numerous skin discs ; some sputum-like bodies ; numerous granulates of the mucous mem-brane ; numerous minute particles of flesh ; traces of ' Sul-phozyansaurem ' potash. The dried residue weighed 8.60 gr. per litre. Three grs. of ash." This researcher was able to detach a small piece of ectoplasm, with the permission of the controlling guide, and this was the analysis : " Colourless, slightly cloudy, fluid (not thready), no smell, traces of cell detritus and sputum. Deposit, whitish. Reaction, slightly alkaline."

After the seance, be it materialization, voice or levitation, the ectoplasm is reabsorbed by the medium, who is invariably very hungry, or in need of some stimulant such as tea, or tobacco. The fact that some mediums need such a stimulant, when they have apparently been in a trance or coma, proves that a physical, as well as an auric, power has been used.

No doubt, as time goes on, we shall learn more of the laws apertaining to these things. The writer does not claim to be an authority on the way in which psychic phenomenon are produced, but submits these few remarks and observations, in all humility, to those people who may know even less, and who desire to know more. Unto all such people I would say : " Salutations to you as you stand on the threshold of the unknown ! Go forward, and time will reveal many wonders, not only in the outer world, but also in your own self ! "

All the teaching that has come from such seances can be summed up in the words " Onward and upward." Set your eyes on the stars of the great ones who have gone before and whose love now draws you up and on in the desire TO KNOW MORE, and whose counsel is always Service ! Service ! and again Service ! Service to God, to humanity, to the spirit world, for all are one and the same now. By loving service we expand our hearts, minds and auras. We transmute the base metals of earthly possessions into the fire of heavenly light. We build ourselves an auric body of power and splendour in which we may later function to the fulness of our capacity, for when we cast off the physical body we shall find ourselves in a spirit body composed of the elements drawn from this same aura, and the light that illumines it will be neither hidden nor darkened ; but if the light be absent, then it can only be created by long years of service on the spirit planes of Being. Now is our opportunity ! Now is our chance, so let us all serve and love and learn, in the hope that we may play our part in creating heaven upon earth !

Selected Titles from the Weiser Backlist

Alder, Vera Stanley. THE FINDING OF THE THIRD EYE
The secret knowledge—secrets of breathing, color, sound, diet, exercise, and how these can be used to develop the third eye. Also a discussion of the dangers on the path to wisdom, and recommendations for the first steps to mastery of the self. 1973. 188 pp. Over 65,000 sold.
ISBN 0-87728-056-8   Paper. $4.95

Alder, Vera Stanley. FROM THE MUNDANE TO THE MAGNIFICENT
According to Ageless Wisdom, humanity is only at the halfway stage of development. Super-development has been demonstrated by saints and sages, but ESP, clairvoyance, clairaudience, psychometry, and healing are all involuntary. We can learn to plug into the wavelengths outside our solar system to help humanity mature. A description of a real-life experience. 1979. 204 pp.
ISBN 0-87728-504-7   Paper. $5.95

Alder, Vera Stanley. WHEN HUMANITY COMES OF AGE
For those who wish to be part of the new age consciousness. Part II prepares you for a new life style. Information about diet, the seven senses, self-healing, mental fitness, self-mastery, choosing a leader. 1972. 226 pp.
ISBN 0-87728-186-6   Paper. $4.95

Bagnall, Oscar. THE ORIGINS & PROPERTIES OF THE HUMAN AURA
Provides a detailed description of the properties of the aura and experimental evidence concerning the particular tissue from which the component parts of the aura originate. Index. 1975. 197 pp.
ISBN 0-87728-284-6   Paper. $3.50

Bennett, J.G. ENNEAGRAM STUDIES
This living diagram is a consciousness device, capable of transforming the person who uses it. Bennett applies the principles of this symbol to everyday situations such as manufacturing, experimenting, working in a kitchen to show that the Enneagram is the key to the very structure of human intelligence. Includes Enneagram of Lord's Prayer in action. 1983. 144 pp.
ISBN 0-87728-544-6   Paper. $5.95

Bennett, J.G. SEX
Sex is a powerful force in our lives, and often a subject avoided by teachers on a spiritual path. Bennett seeks to answer questions that are asked by students of spiritual growth—such questions as Is there any connection between sex and spirituality? What is sex for? What effects do men and women have on each other sexually? His guidance can help men and women better understand and appreciate each other. 1981. 74 pp.
ISBN 0-87728-533-0   Paper. $4.95

Bennett, J.G. THE WAY TO BE FREE
The lectures that are the foundation for this book were given at Sherborne House in the last years before Bennett died in 1974. The material can be used as a handbook for beginners, who are sometimes suspicious or afraid of more abstruse works on spiritual matters. This book will also provide food for thought for more advanced students on the path. 1980. 208 pp.
ISBN 0-87728-491-1   Paper. $6.95

Bias, Clifford. RITUAL BOOK OF MAGIC
This is a working guide to magic and rituals for the beginner or advanced practitioner. Rituals include Exorcism, Love Philtres, Planetary Magic, Talismans, a Private Temple Rite, and more. 1981. 125 pp.
ISBN 0-87728-532-2   Paper. $5.95

Brennan, J.H. ASTRAL DOORWAYS
Provides concentration and visualization exercises to prepare the reader for an astral journey through one of the four doors. 1972. 115 pp.
ISBN 0-85030-242-0   Paper. $6.95

Brunton, Paul. DISCOVER YOURSELF
Finding your own spiritual center and path in an era when education stresses outer values while forgetting the inner drives. Psycho-spiritual self-analysis helps you use your own mind to delve into spiritual matters. 1971. Revised paper edition 1983. 244 pp. (Formerly titled: *Inner Reality.*)
ISBN 0-87728-592-6   Paper. $7.95

Brunton, Paul. A HERMIT IN THE HIMALAYAS
The journal of a sojourn in India, living with holy men, sharing the mysteries of the East, reflections about yoga and meditation, as well as the personal search for inner peace. 1971. Revised paper edition 1984. 188 pp.
ISBN 0-87728-601-9   Paper. $6.95

Brunton, Paul. THE HIDDEN TEACHING BEYOND YOGA
What is the meaning of the world? What am I? What is the object of my existence? Deeds can never be greater than ideas, and to cure our own or the world's sorrows, ignorance will have to be replaced by the hidden knowledge. 1972. Revised edition 1984. 366 pp.
ISBN 0-87728-590-X   Paper. $8.95

Brunton, Paul. THE QUEST OF THE OVERSELF
Analysis of the physical, emotional, and intellectual self. Part II is a discussion of the spiritual development that can take place—including instruction about the practice of mental mastery; the path of self-inquiry; mysteries surrounding breath, eye, heart, overself. 1970. Revised paper edition 1984. 240 pp.
ISBN 0-87728-594-2   Paper. $7.95

Brunton, Paul. A SEARCH IN SECRET EGYPT
The story of Brunton's visit to Egypt, the pyramids, spending a night in a pyramid, the relationship between Egyptian culture and the memory of Atlantis. Interviews with Tahra Bey, Egypt's most famour fakir. 1970. New paper edition 1984. 288 pp.
ISBN 0-87728-603-5   Paper. $7.95

Brunton, Paul. A SEARCH IN SECRET INDIA
The story of the search in India for the spirituality of the ages, sharing the sights and sounds of India as Westerners hear of it, and looking for the spiritual haven he knew was there. 1970. Revised paper edition 1984. 314 pp.
ISBN 0-87728-602-7   Paper. $8.95

Brunton, Paul. THE SPIRITUAL CRISIS OF MAN
The plight of mankind, the chaos caused by technological and scientific discoveries, the spiritual emptiness, are discussed here. The voice of the soul, the power of intuition, are what Dr. Brunton feels links God with people and talks about how this can be done. 1972. Revised paper edition, 1984. 224 pp.
ISBN 0-87728-593-4   Paper. $7.95

Brunton, Paul. THE WISDOM OF THE OVERSELF
The spiritual value of sleep and dreams, the nature and function of personality in the process of evolution, development of intuition to draw people closer to the Universal Mind. Meditation and its practical applications to modern society. 1969. Revised paper edition 1984. 376 pp.
ISBN 0-87728-591-8   Paper. $8.95

Chu, W.K. and Sherrill, W.A. THE ASTROLOGY OF I CHING
This volume is based on the same concepts and derivations as the I Ching. Both books share in ageless Chinese knowledge and philosophy. But here we also have the application of the Celestial Stems and Horary Branches as a basis for determining the appropriate natal hexagram with its controlling line and the subsequent evolvement into yearly and daily predictions. First English translation of the 'Ho Map Lo Map Rational Number' manuscript. Charts. Index. 1976. First paper edition 1980. 443 pp.
ISBN 0-87728-492-X   Paper. $9.95

Crawford, Quantz. METHODS OF PSYCHIC DEVELOPMENT
The basics of psychic development. Exercises to open the psychic centers, techinques for controlling and using the new powers you develop. Dr. Crawford is an effective and well-known teacher. Illustrated. 1983. 102 pp.
ISBN 0-87728-545-4   Paper. $5.95

D'Agostino, Joseph D. TAROT—THE ROYAL PATH TO WISDOM
Using the Waite deck as a basis, D'Agostino delineates the meditative symbolism inherent in each of the 22 cards of the Greater Arcana and explains the use of the Tarot as a means of divination. 1977. 132 pp.
ISBN 0-87728-329-X   Paper. $2.95

Ferguson, Sibyl.THE CRYSTAL BALL
This little essay contains a short history of the crystal ball, instructions on its housing and use, how to read the crystal, the interpretation of phenomena seen and a bibliography. 1980. 16 pp.
ISBN 0-87728-483-0   Paper. $1.50

Fortune, Dion. APPLIED MAGIC
The practical application of magical and occult techniques. 1973. 110 pp.
ISBN 0-85030-218-8   Paper. $6.95

Fortune, Dion. ASPECTS OF OCCULTISM
Nine essays, each illuminating a different aspect of occultism, as well as an epilogue to **Moon Magic**. 1973. 88 pp.
ISBN 0-87728-385-0   Paper. $5.95

Fortune, Dion. THE COSMIC DOCTRINE
An analysis of cosmic forces acting on humanity and the operation of certain occult laws. 1976. 157 pp.
ISBN 0-87728-455-5   . Paper. $6.95

Fortune, Dion. THE ESOTERIC PHILOSOPHY OF LOVE AND MARRIAGE
Detailed account of the esoteric doctrines relating to sex. 1975. 96 pp.
ISBN 0-85030-121-1   Paper. $5.95

Fortune, Dion. THE MYSTICAL QABALAH
A thorough and systematic analysis of the Ancient Wisdom expressed in the symbolism of the Tree of Life, the glyph that inherently summarizes the yoga of the west. 3 diagrams. 1984. 311 pp.
ISBN 0-87728-596-9   Paper. $6.95

Fortune, Dion. PRACTICAL OCCULTISM IN DAILY LIFE
Explains the theory of reincarnation, the use of mind power, and how to control environment. 1972. First paper edition 1976. 66 pp.
ISBN 0-85030-133-5   Paper. $5.95

Fortune, Dion. PSYCHIC SELF DEFENSE
Practical instructions for the detection of psychic attacks and defence against them. 1971. First paper edition 1977. 209 pp.
ISBN 0-87728-381-8   Paper. $6.95

Fortune, Dion. SANE OCCULTISM
Defines occultism and charts the pitfalls and safeguards encountered in its study and practice. 1973. 192 pp.
ISBN 0-85030-105-X   Paper. $7.95

Fortune, Dion. THROUGH THE GATES OF DEATH
Reveals the guarded knowledge of the Mysteries. 1972. 94 pp.
ISBN 0-85030-091-6 $5.95

Fortune, Dion. THE TRAINING AND WORK OF AN INITIATE
Together with **Esoteric Orders and Their Work** covers the whole field of initiation upon the Right-hand Path of the Western Tradition. 1973. 125 pp.
ISBN 0-85030-154-8   Paper. $6.95

Galante, Lawrence. TAI CHI: THE SUPREME ULTIMATE
Contents include a study of the origins and history of the Hard and Soft Schools of Tai Chi; a detailed analysis of the philosophy of Tai Chi, its relationship to western philosophy, the *I Ching* and the *Tao te Ching*, to Yoga and Zen, and to occult systems, health and Chinese medicine. The second part of the book is on self-defense and contains several hundred photographs showing each and every breath (inhale and exhale) and the application of all moves. Bibliography. Illustrated. 1981. 208 pp.
ISBN 0-87728-497-0   Paper. $9.95

Gilbert, Mitchell. AN OWNER'S MANUAL FOR THE HUMAN BEING
The author, an award winning journalist and radio commentator, has travelled extensively in Asia and the Middle East, always searching for wisdom and truth. This book, based on the teachings of Guru Bawa Muhaiyaddeen, is about "putting one foot in front of the other and actually going to that place of true realization toward which all the prophets have been pointing."
1980. 128 pp.
ISBN 0-87728-496-2   Paper. $4.95

Gray, Wm. G. THE LADDER OF LIGHTS
A step-by-step guide to the Tree of Life and Four Worlds of the Qabalists.
1981. 230 pp.
ISBN 0-87728-536-5   Paper. $7.95

Gray, Wm. G. AN OUTLOOK ON OUR INNER WESTERN WAY
Gray shows simply and lucidly how to *live* the Western Inner Tradition. Tracing the cosmology of Western Magic, he substantiates its vitality and urgency for our future. Not since *Magick in Theory and Practice* and the works of Dion Fortune has there been such a mammoth attempt at presenting Magic as the relevant, living tradition it is. 1980. 160 pp.
ISBN 0-87728-493-8   Paper $6.95

Gray, Wm. G. SANGREAL SACRAMENT
Volume 2 of the Sangreal Sodality Series, a home study course in magic. An exploration of the meaning of the sangreal symbol, the power generated by visualization, chanting, the celebration of the sacrament, how to create a personal stronghold, nature of true contemplation, how to seek your own personal sangreal. Illustrated. 1983. 224 pp.
ISBN 0-87728-562-4   Paper. $8.95

Gray, Wm G. A SELF MADE BY MAGIC
Gray deals with the spiritual significance of "self," setting out the entire problem of self-approach and individual evolution according to initiated Magical procedures. 1974. First paper edition 1984. 198 pp.
ISBN 0-87728-556-X   Paper. $8.95

Gray, Wm. G. THE TALKING TREE
This work explores the living Archetypes of the Tree of Life and their relation to the daily work of the practicing Occultist. 1977. First paper edition 1981. 583 pp.
ISBN 0-87728-537-3   Paper. $12.50

Gray, Wm. G. WESTERN INNER WORKINGS
Volume 1 of the Sangreal Sodality Series, a home study course in magic. Provides step-by-step instructions for training consciousness in the Western Tradition. Included is morning meditation, mid-day invocation, evening exercises, questions for the student. Illustrated. 1983. 272 pp.
ISBN 0-87728-560-8   Paper. $8.95

Hansen, Harold. THE WITCH'S GARDEN
Discusses the plants used by witches down through the ages and how they carried on the practice of herbal medicine. Some of the plants discussed are mandrake, deadly nightshade, hemlock, witches' flying ointments, etc. 1983. 128 pp.
ISBN 0-87728-551-9   Paper. $5.95

Johnson, Vera Scott, and Wommack, Thomas. THE SECRETS OF NUMBERS
A numerological Guide to Your Character and Destiny. A presentation in workbook format of the major systems of numerology. Undocumented new systems and interpretations. Illustrated. Charts. 1982. 257 pp.
ISBN 0-87728-541-1   8½ x 11 Paper. $12.50

Kargere, Audrey. COLOR AND PERSONALITY
The study of color is based on the research findings of scientists and psychologists going back as far as the days of Egypt, Babylon, India and China. Includes chapter on the human aura, the physical effects of colors, personality and character analysis through color, chromotherapy and much more. Charts. Glossary. Index. 1979. 144 pp.
ISBN 0-87728-478-4   Paper. $4.95

Kilner, W.J. THE AURA
Pioneer researches on viewing the human aura. Foreword by Sibyl Ferguson.
Index. Illustrated. 1973. 331 pp. Over 30,000 sold.
ISBN 0-87728-215-3   Paper. $3.95

Lawson-Wood, D. & J. THE INCREDIBLE HEALING NEEDLES
This is a layman's guide to Chinese Acupuncture. Diagrams. 1975. 73 pp.
ISBN 0-87728-298-6   Paper. $1.25

Love, Jeff. THE QUANTUM GODS
The Quantum Gods are beings of infinite ability. Yet each of them exists alone,
unconscious of the existence of the others and unable to manifest as a creative
being. This is not a science fiction fantasy. The Quantum Gods are not ghosts,
angels or beings from another planet or time zone. This is a work of radical
metaphysical philosophy unlike any other. You and I are the Quantum Gods.
Illustrated. 1979. 242 pp.
ISBN 0-87728-476-8   Paper. $7.95

MacIvor, Virginia & LaForest, Sandra. VIBRATIONS:
HEALING THROUGH COLOR, HOMEOPATHY AND RADIONICS
An authoritative treatment of the holistic approach to the art and science of
natural healing. MacIvor and LaForest draw syncretically from both Western
and Eastern medical traditions as well as on investigations, experiences and
technology of contemporary practitioners. Abounds in critical and visual apparatus, charts, color keys, diagrams, illustrations and exhaustive
bibliographic references. 1979. 180 pp.
ISBN 0-87728-393-i   Paper. $6.95

Muldoon, S., and Carrington, H. THE PROJECTION OF THE ASTRAL BODY
Instructions on the specific methods for bringing about the projection of the
astral body as well as many experiences. Index. 1968. 319 pp.
ISBN 0-87728-069-X   Paper. $5.95

Ophiel. THE ART AND PRACTICE OF ASTRAL PROJECTION
Gives all the necessary theory and directions to enter the Astral plane, func-
tion there, and return with the memory available. 1961. 123 pp.
ISBN 0-87728-246-3   Paper. $5.95

Ophiel. THE ART AND PRACTICE OF CABALLA MAGIC
Ophiel's seventh book provides clear instructions for practical, productive
work using the symbols of the Tree of Life in daily life.
Color Plates. Illustrated. 1977. 152 pp.
ISBN 0-87728-303-6   Paper. $5.95

Ophiel. THE ART AND PRACTICE OF CLAIRVOYANCE
Provides the best knowledge required to understand and use this natural power inherent in all people. Illustrated. 1969. 138 pp.
ISBN 0-87728-325-7   Paper. $5.95

Ophiel. THE ART AND PRACTICE OF GETTING MATERIAL THINGS THROUGH CREATIVE VISUALIZATION
Techniques for entering the Inner Planes to create favorable circumstances for yourself in the outer or Physical Plane. Illustrated. 1967. 120 pp.
ISBN 0-87728-588-8   Paper. RPT

Papon, Donald. THE LURE OF THE HEAVENS
This authoritative work traces the origins and development of astrology through thousands of years and many civilizations. Here is astrology as the world's oldest science, as an ancient universal religion, as man's first majestic effort toward cosmic understanding and as a study of human character and consciousness. Illustrated. Glossary. Bibliography. Index. 1980. 320 pp.
ISBN 0-87728-502-0   Paper. $7.95

Popoff, Irmis B. GURDJIEFF GROUP WORK WITH WILHEM NYLAND
A verbatim look at the most vital tool for disseminating Gurdjieff's teachings—the working group. Sessions with teacher Nyland, as a memorial to his life, for he was one of the followers appointed to carry on the Work. 1983. 80 pp.
ISBN 0-87728-580-2   Paper. 4.95

Ravenscroft, Trevor. THE CUP OF DESTINY
The author takes us to the heart of the legend of the Holy Grail, showing its meaning for mankind. Parallels to faiths other than Christianity, particularly in cases of Buddhism, Zoroastrianism and Manichaeism. 1982. 194 pp.
ISBN 0-87728-546-2   Paper. $6.95

Ravenscroft, Trevor. THE SPEAR OF DESTINY
The occult power behind the spear which pierced the side of Christ. . .and how Hitler inverted the Force in a bid to conquer the world. 1982. 362 pp.
ISBN 0-87728-547-0   Paper. $8.50

Regardie, Israel. THE ONE YEAR MANUAL
This is a twelve-month manual to bring the serious student of consciousness to an ongoing awareness of unity. Originally published under the title Twelve Steps To Spiritual Enlightenment, Dr. Regardie has revised this edition to progress from the physical disciplines of body-awareness, relaxation, and rhythmic breathing, through concentration, developing the will, mantra-practice, to the ultimate awareness that All is God.
Bibliography. Revised edition 1981. 77 pp.
ISBN 0-87728-301-X   Paper. $4.95

Regardie, Israel. A PRACTICAL GUIDE TO GEOMANTIC DIVINATION
(Paths to Inner Power Series.) This is a guide for the serious student who wants to enhance his extrasensory perception, thereby gaining a living sense of the rhythms of growth, blooming, and decay. 1972. 64 pp.
ISBN 0-87728-170-X   Paper. $2.50

Rice, Paul and Valeta. THRU THE NUMBERS
The authors have written twelve separate booklets, one for each sun sign, teaching beginners how to do numerology while comparing the value of numbers to the qualities of the astrological sun signs. 1983. 40 pp. ea.
ISBN 0-87728-605-1   Paper. $2.00 ea.

Wang, Robert. INTRODUCTION TO THE GOLDEN DAWN TAROT
The publication of this book coincides with the release, by Dr. Israel Regardie, of the Golden Dawn Tarot Deck which has been shrouded in 80 years of secrecy, and has now been painted under his personal supervision by Dr. Robert Wang. Dr. Wang has written an excellent introduction which highlights the Order teachings which are included in the text. Reading list. 1978. 158 pp.
ISBN 0-87728-370-2   Paper. $6.95

Wang, Robert. THE QABALISTIC TAROT
A textbook of mystical philosophy. Hailed by reviewers as the most significant work on Tarot to appear in twenty years—this complex study demonstrates how to use the tarot for inner development. It explains the Hermetic Qabalah in terms of the Waite, Marseilles, Crowley and Golden Dawn decks. Illustrated. Index. 1983. 304 pp.
ISBN 0-87728-520-9   7 x 10 Cloth. $22.50

Wirth, Oswald. INTRODUCTION TO THE STUDY OF THE TAROT
English translation of a French edition published in 1889. Foreword by Stuart Kaplan. Wirth was a central figure in the history of tarot and tarot design, having an extensive knowledge of occult symbolism. This basic primer relates the 22 major arcana to esoteric symbolism, showing how cards can help develop dreams that energize the cards.
Illustrated. Accompanies the Wirth Tarot Deck. 1983. 64 pp.
ISBN 0-87728-559-4   Paper. $4.95

Young, Ellin Dodge & Schuler, Carol. THE VIBES BOOK
It's fun! A simple way to learn about yourself, love, sex, career, money, desires . . . THE VIBES BOOK is a step-by-step numerology workbook with easy to follow instructions and includes all necessary reference material and worksheets. Charts. Calendars. Bibliography. 1979. 129 pp.
ISBN 0-87728-414-8   Paper. $5.95